cameo diner

MATT MILLER

cameo diner

POEMS

LOOM PRESS
2 0 0 5
Lowell, Massachusetts

Cameo Diner
Copyright © 2005 by Matt Miller

ISBN 0-931507-14-6

Printed in the United States of America
First Edition

Designer: Victoria Dalis
Photographer: Meghan Moore
Typeface: Caslon text with Copperplate and John Doe display
Printer: Thomson-Shore, Inc.

Loom Press
P.O. Box 1394
Lowell, Massachusetts 01853
www.loompress.com
editor@loompress.com

for Emily and Delaney

c ontents

III. WINTER SEEDS

introduction

Lowell, Massachusetts, home of the poet Matt Miller, was once a great industrial center—a place which, along with the other mill towns of the Northeast, helped lift the American economy to dizzying heights. The mill owners of the nineteenth and twentieth centuries made their fortunes on the backs of the workers—often young women. The workers put in fourteen-hour days, then promptly paid much of their small wages back to the mill owners for rent in the nearby corporate boarding-houses.

The mill buildings are compelling places to visit now, at the beginning of this new century. They have been redesigned and refitted as malls to house small shops and restaurants and medical offices—the bricks sandblasted, the floors refinished and glistening with urethane. Often you will see old mill machines displayed at the entrance to these places, strange dinosaurs that once represented American promise and genius. Walking within the buildings is, for me, disconcerting—thinking of the people who worked in these cavernous rooms, how they must, in quick moments, have looked out the large windows with yearning, at sky, river, brick. There is a soul to these old mills that all of the sandblasting in the world cannot touch—the ghost of human yearning and dignity is still here, a conscience asking for recognition.

The work of Matt Miller is full of this thing called conscience. This is not a writer pining for a stint on a famous talk show, or eager to "network" to find out about the next literary contest that might give him a glimpse of recognition. Matt writes, as a fellow Merrimack Valley writer, Andre Dubus, once described it, "into the silence of mortality"—into the mystery of what it is to be human, with our annihilation always a possibility, with our determination always plucking us up from despair. How is it that human beings survive, the poet seems to ask, with so much madness about, so much danger—so much impulse on the part of the powerful to use the next human being as part of an agenda?

When Matt writes of Lowell, or of California, or of his college town of New Haven, the ghosts of the past are always in his words, breathing, surviving, making the best of it; the geography itself is also a character that hovers, a history waiting to be discovered and paid homage to. From his booth in a Lowell diner the poet writes:

> outside in the millbrick midnight, the canals
> > of the Merrimack
> run red in the blood glow of brake lights.

What I love about Matt Miller's work is that he makes me see, afresh, the mill towns of New England that I have also called home—to see the wide Merrimack River and the tall weeds by railroad tracks and the 6:15 commuter train that "hunches toward Boston"; the abandoned mills and shops and the brightly-lit diners by night and the hooker named Flowers and the worker with forearms "three days dirty and lashed thick with veins." I love the timelessness of his descriptions and how, in his hand, ghosts usually forgotten become immortal.

Joseph Campbell tells us, in his *The Inner Reaches of Outer Space*, that writing was born in Mesopotamia during the fourth millennium BC, as man began looking beyond what was local. "The leap was from geography to the cosmos," Campbell writes, "beyond the moon, whereupon the primal, limited and limiting tribal manner of thought…was by the Gentile civilizations left behind. That was the period when writing was invented; also, mathematical measurement, and the wheel."

Here in these pages, on a cold, New Haven night close to dawn, the writer comes across a black woman desperate for money; she is willing to barter some small part of what she has left of soul or body for relief. Matt's sadness for her, his heart going out to her, transcends geography: we might be in a communist land during the Stalin years; we might be in South Africa during the time of Apartheid, or in the American South of the nineteen-fifties. We might be in ancient

Rome, or watching the woman beg on a street in Mesopotamia six thousand years ago.

> *I'd seen her before, begging rocks under*
> *the alley light of my building. Fat, black,*
> *and teeth that looked like they were knocked around*
> *by a pipe, she stopped me on my steps, a thick*
> *sweater (recently abandoned by moths and mice)*
> *keeping her warm in New Haven's chill.*

This is the writer's job—to make us feel for all of humanity, at all times, through the description of one time. To make us see the ghosts of old and the ghosts of now. To haunt us.

I met Matt Miller when he was a student of mine in the MFA program at Boston's Emerson College. Matt stands tall, with the build of his famous grandfather, Raymond E. Riddick, who played for the Green Bay Packers. He has eyes that might be described as shy— he is not a type to call attention to himself—but are also at turns full of empathy and determination and humor. He has a strong sense of chivalry—rare in young men now—and seems to read everything he can get his hands on. He had a great interest, I remember, in writers of his region, Kerouac and Dubus, and in how these artists transcended their surroundings. There are certain students—you come across one or two of them every ten years—who have an unusual mixture of talent and experience, and whose writing seems to rise off the page as you first read it, a voice announcing I am here. Matt was such a student. I watched with pride as he wrote prose (without much help from me) that I knew would be published; I watched him get his degree and his first teaching jobs (his students, responding to his honesty, love him). I was there when he married his wonderful Emily, (a formal ceremony in Newburyport, Massachusetts, another old mill town), and I happily got an ecstatic e-mail from him when Emily gave birth to their first child. He has recently been nominated for the Pushcart Prize, and won a prestigious Stegner Fellowship—an honor which will send him to Stanford for twenty months. To this young writer who does not campaign for recognition, rewards are coming for hard work and a compassionate, wise eye.

And now this fine book. You hold in your hands the work of a writer the world will know. I invite you, proudly, to be haunted with me.

Joseph Hurka
August, 2005

I. two-stroke engine mix

THE BLADES

for Walshy and Mitch

From the dark concrete gape of a rented garage,
across a New England dust and heat August,
as the 6:15 commuter rail sighs past the tall weeds
and rusted box cars of Gallagher Terminal
and hunches south toward Boston, a wail of dying
metal crows the morning out from under its own
shadows—a landscaper sharpening the blades
of his mowers against an electric sander's bony
spin. Sparks wasp across forearms, which are three
days dirty and lashed thick with veins. He stiffens,
gliding the blades back and forth to rub from
yesterday's dulled brown this morning's sharp cut
of silver. A Marlboro hangs from his bottom lip unlit
as his eyes become buried in the rhythm. He forgets
the press of sweat, the pain in his back, the bills
and the billings, the iced coffee melting in the pickup.
Forgets it all just long enough to get lost in the whine
of the blades as they pass under the wheel. Until
the sharpening is done. Then with a torque wrench
he tightens the blades back onto the mowers,
changes the air filters, loads them onto the trailer
along with shovels, rakes, saws, and backpack blowers
and heads out for the rows. The rows of old women
always late to pay, of young mothers who want just
one more thing cut, of men who will do a better job
when they have the time. The rows of angry corners,
lawn ornaments, painted mulch, hive husks, and stones.
The rows upon rows that he must cut before the day
wears out and dulls into dark behind the roofed hills.

THE YUCCA HUNTERS

Mornings in Baja grunt heat like a pregnant hog
clumping full-titted through the dust and shit
of a Puenta Colonette patio. My steps tangle

as I cross the scrubs of vegetation. The breaths
of angry ghosts press down on my naked back
and this garbage yard desert of abandoned time,

tin shack churches, and lizards waiting in
the sand, patient for our outcome. Booted
and gloved against the wide lances of leaves I rip

another summer-dead shrub of yucca
out of the earth. With their long center stems
and wide drooping leaves they look like Lorax

trees, or that's what I'm thinking as I haul
four of them back to the pickup truck, stomping
over the rattlers and scorpions that rumor

in the cacti, a plug of Red Man snug inside
my cheek. I heave the yuccas one by one
onto the pile already stacked ten feet high

in the Chevy's bed. Alone in the sky the sun
furnaces with hate. I wipe dirt from my face
and watch the others drag their catches back

across the sizzle that dizzies my vision, and I
can't imagine the need for the fire these plants
will keep alive. But this is the desert, and

it will turn cold. Winds will blow off the coast,
rumbling waves over the shipwrecking rocks,
the Pacific howling at the animals

she spat upon the earth. Night will sing
the flames to dance across the piles of yucca
as we set fire to the dark, circle in echoes

of whalebones, conch shells, and surf boards.
Slurping down greasy chunks of smoke-cooked pork,
we'll bury bottles of wine and beer, leaning

back from the blaze, cross-legged in the sand,
swirling constellations with our hands,
our voices coyoted up to a July 4th moon.

THE PIN MONKEY

A bent-over crowd all half in the bag
on "50 Cent Draft Night" at Garnsie's Lanes
in Joliet, near Statesville's hum of electric lockup,
as an old man pushes into a barstool, fingernails
a scab into a deeper scar, whistles for a drink
through his three-ten split of teeth, and jingles
a plastic baggie of quarters against the hum of balls
rolling thunder down planes of varnish into
the thick-necked echoes of candlepins that shrapnel
the lanes and maintain a perfected white noise
of collision, while on the TV the Cubs are losing
again as spirits are rationed out in stingy pours
by a barkeep munching pretzels and stealing bills
from a waitress with flat hair and menthol perfume,
who sifts her hips through tables of leers and sweaty
grips, lining up drinks for five bucks an hour
plus tips, not even enough for her to afford a sitter
as her boy john henrys a back wall video game,
playing all night on one quarter, and again across
the bar the old man slides his coins for another fill,
faces this babel with a fractured grin and yells,
"I used to set these fucking pins by hand!"

PISCATORY DINER

I'm squeezed behind Formica and chrome, sitting in a diner booth
waiting for my steak and eggs, spitting tobacco into an empty Coke can,

and scratching some words on a paper napkin,
just hoping to hook a rhythm on stale bait while

outside in the millbrick midnight, the canals of the Merrimack
run red in the blood glow of brake lights.

Casting my lines across these city veins where carp slip in the muck
among blown tires, immigrant bones, and the used-up breath of

all of us bottom-feeding for meaning, I try
to fishplate this downtown mise en scène

of a hooker named Flowers sucking glass dick in an alley,
then stiletto-stepping through the parking lot

where a couple stumbles toward their car from the Worthen bar,
their tongues tangled as they lean against a burnt-out street light

while two kids hooded in gang rags slide like cobras
into the diner, smoking butts and taking stools in the corner

near Jimmy Sullivan, the old bantam weight whose sauced body
bobs and weaves over a half-eaten turkey sandwich

served by a waitress walking under nicotine halos
who smiles through too much makeup at me going hungry

as a hairnetted cook throws baking soda on a grease fire
that shuts down the grill for the night.

PERISCOPE

I've hoisted gods on my shoulders before
and so you've probably seen them dancing
above the crowd, effortlessly gliding over
the human sea like sweaty kids dumb-faced at
a July parade. I'm big and tall though so it's
really no effort and really gods are actually
quite light, much lighter than you'd think, bones
like birds I guess, and I apologize if I ever confused
anyone or caused a cult or worse a religion, it's just
that as tall as I am I hoped to see a little further
but male or female, dog or cat, savior or trickster
or whatever combination thereof it was all
a waste of effort since once sprung forth or
pulled out from my squinting brow
and thrown up onto my back, they all turned out
to be blind, every last one of them.

HIERARCHY OF PARADISE

Far north the mortar of gutted cotton
mills, up a river's long dark mane
of whispers, high into the hills'
old oak and pine, September wades
up to its shoulders in milk. Waking

into midnight, boulders glisten,
quick waters fill with assignments
of lightning and ponds bleach out like sheets.
Swishing silver in breezes the trees
sway lightly into the west. Except

for one leaf, one sagging palm of sugar
maple bending low from the prayer
and perch of a mantis that watches and waits
to pounce on third shift foragers.
And then he sees, emerging from creek

bank muds, a digger wasp in hunt
of larvae in which to suckle her brood.
She rises ragged up and into
the air. Her legs are trampled stems
beneath her. Fumbling through the leaves

she never sees his bent shadow.
Black angles thicken above her. Arms
unfold their spikes. They tear and crush
her, then raise her as if in supplication
to a moon already filling with bats.

GRAVEDIGGERS UNION

Beneath the feathered blades of November ash
I cut across a Nashua graveyard, past
the stone-pillowed rows stuck with little flags.
The fog and cold bury the sun. Glancing

over the names of fallen vets, it occurs
to me that all the books, the leads, the streams
of video feed have never shown me or told
me about the gravediggers of Baghdad. But I

imagine they must be thick across the back,
thicknecked from so many prolific seasons
of sowing. Their hands must be as rough and hard
as shovel handles, and their legs like taut

ship's hemp and swollen with blood. To see them work,
to see their lean bodies bend into the earth
must be the pure ideal of our human machine.
Until, that is, you get a little closer,

enough to see that their backs will never again
be straight. To know those necks are spades that will
always be shoved by dust into dust. To know
that if you get close enough to smell the sick

that reaches over their loose-toothed laughter
you'll realize that their eyes have long since sewn
themselves shut against eternity. And I,
still reading names beneath the autumn ash,

bend down to pull a flag from out of the grass.
And then I stop. Still bent. Still penitent
as a fleshy breeze gnaws into my back
and nudges another digger on his way.

ALL THE DIFFERENCE

While walking home at night just scratching dawn's
hairy belly, the smell of wet dogwood
and hot-top in the air and my boots wobbly
over the cracks of Elm Street, I met a girl.

I'd seen her before, begging rocks under
the alley light of my building. Fat, black,
with teeth that looked like they were knocked around
by a pipe, she stopped me on my steps, a thick

sweater (recently abandoned by moths and mice)
keeping her warm in New Haven's April chill.
I looked at the purple cakes that were her eyes,
said something like Yes? or, Yeah? when she asked

me what I was doing right then. I told her I
was going to sleep, at which she started to pull
away her sweater where it buttoned in
the front, revealing her breasts draping tattered

and free under a t-shirt rolled up to just
below her throat. I stared at their sagging
nudity, their large dark nipples, the swollen
stomach they stretched to rest upon. *This could*

help you sleep, she said. Hinges squeaked inside
my mind like a churchyard gate blown by
an October wind. I tried to think. I tried
not to think. I finally answered, *No thanks,*

I'm really tired, and turned and walked up the steps,
and rumbled through the door and glad for once
someone forgot to lock it last night. Then risking
the salt, I paused. I looked back, hindsight being

what it is, and saw her through a window,
still standing there, her back to me, her head
moving up and down the street as if watching
for a late bus, and for a moment I did

consider letting her up, bringing her
to bed, fucking her. And then even letting
her fall asleep. At least until morning.
At least until the grinding of gears and cables

opened the elevator door and hollowed
me out with thoughts of blood and wallet.
Instead, I rode up to my apartment, tripped
through the door, and passed out on the couch.

CONJUNCTION

A day caked in rust and hooded in the blue
blonde grind of a man and woman both angry-
hearted for the East as they drive their Bronco
mute through a southern Utah afternoon.

They've been wordless since Vegas.

                                 Even
here—

        as they roll up on a strange arrangement
of blood and fur frescoed onto the desert blacktop
by some recent crush of grill and tires, and now
being reworked in drip and splash by the rip
and tear of some turkey-vulture Pollock—

they are still silent.

                  The dead-eyed stag stares out
across the serrated orange hills that scrape a cloudless
indigo.

           With a hollow sound of crushed sand
and pebble the Bronco rolls to the shoulder
of Route 17 and brakes for death.

                        Scowling,
the vulture scatters from his art as out
of the dust that billows from under the idling
truck step man and woman.

Carrying
disposable cameras, quiet as decay they
walk towards the body of the deer.

Only
the wind and click of plastic eyes shatter
the air.

They take in the heat, the flies,
the unrestrained stink of the day until
still without words,

their memento caught
and boxed, they return to their truck and bottled
waters.

They drive away.

Heat lightning licks
the road that their eyes have followed for so many
hours,

a road that has held them for so many
miles

in a swollen hush of blood and tongue.

THE FLORIST

A winter rain rivers down Gorham Street
gutters the slush and trash and drags a sprig
of holly past the sub shops and liquor stores,
skipping it over ice and past potholes,

until the flooding water pools and purls
in front of an iron grate, a moment swirling,
then spilling the holly into the dark below a flower
shop where an old woman balances above

an icy puddle as she unlocks the gate
and then the front door. Morning's eternity
announced by a bell jingling above. She pushes
into the store and gets caught in the bloom of rose

and daffodil and their thick scents of earth.
She walks behind the counter. She opens up
the register, checks any orders, puts out
the holiday displays and begins to pot

arrangements. Eyeglasses hang against her
breasts on a beaded plastic chain roped around
her neck. She waits on a thinning parade
of customers. For lunch she has tuna-on-rye,

watches her shows, and tries to reach her son
by phone. That afternoon she walks across
the street to the cemetery and places a wreath
by her husband's stone. An evening rush of two

men needing to buy a dozen each, then she brings
in the displays, closes the register, locks the door
and the gate. She walks against the pins of rain,
reaching the Buick as blue deepens between

leafless branches. She pulls out into the stream
of taillights, headlights, and streetlights that blur
beyond the windshield corners. She feels a tug
as the street now drags her down into the dark.

THE PLOWS

Like trick ink into a sketch diary,
this town of mills and bridges fades
into the blink of morning that an ice

storm has left behind. The river cricks
arthritically with floes that rub
cozy as lovers against each other.

Icicles fang from power lines,
from maples and pines that creak and clink.
Upon their pikes are impaled the ghosts

that haunt alleys and garbage cans
with groans of winter. Thick chunks
of ice are scattered in the streets

like teeth busted loose from brawling
frost giants and which no one has bothered
to sweep up. Until, that is, the trucks,

muscled by big Detroits, rumble
their diesel hearts out of park, hubs locked,
clutches grinding. Grunting behind

diamond-plated plows they shake. They scrape
the daybreak raw of quiet and ice.
Throwing off sparks, they tear concrete

from out under the silver glow of lanes,
avenues, empty lots, and two-
car driveways. Iron shovels

furrow through crystal. Buckets dump
their salt and sand. The sleepers wake
from under cotton tents to a dawn

choking gasoline through their windows.
Gears shift for torque. The gray and hard
begins to grid across the town

as the plows crush out the glowing pearl
of snow that had thrown up its light,
for a few hours, against the horizon.

II. the dust in our cells

MECHANICS

Too warm to need the fire, we build
it anyway if only to sit
and watch it die. Beyond its glow
the campsite sleeps. The woods are draped

in tar, and you lean toward the fire.
Taking long drags on your Lucky Strikes,
you flick the mechanics of your Bic
and sigh blue smoke through your false teeth.

Hunched into shadow and knife,
I whittle sticks into snakes and squint
against the weakening light. Beers
sit half empty and warm beside

us. The nervous purpose of this.
As if our hands are desperate
to fill the mute we've cradled here.
You with your lighter and I my knife,

hunting again the words. But we've
never sifted a language from the coals.
Perhaps we assume that we are men
and that it doesn't matter. Flames

leap like lunatics from the logs and lick
yellow against your glasses. Tinder pops
with gas and spits the cinders that
we kick back in before they can burn out.

COLORING

The color "flesh" is voluntarily changed to "peach" in 1962 partially as the result of the U.S. Civil Rights movement.

—*from* Crayola.com

Skinny like the saw blades of grass that shoot
out of the dunes, my brother Jon ran long
across the beach for a bomb. His stick arms swung
out of synch with his Indian-red jersey, his feet

pumped through the haze and the sun-baked sand.
Sand that was once yellow until a birthday
had brought a bigger box of Crayolas,
and stained the sand with shades of maize and tan.

Shaggy hair, once brown but now mahogany,
was blown like flames in a breeze as he galloped.
I reached back with the swollen football and launched
it as far as my rag arm could, through wobbly

spirals across the sky-blue sky and the lemon-
yellow sun. A terrible throw, the ball was way
off mark, and it landed thudding and bouncing by
a group of older boys walking along

a sea-green Atlantic that sparkled with new gold
and silver. Jon, not missing a beat, cut right
down the slope of the beach to shag the ball. Despite
him being half as big and half as old

as these other kids, he was fearless, and ran
right over to them, one of whom was a tall
wide-shouldered kid our dad would call
black, but really he was colored more an

umber or raw sienna. He bent down
and picked the ball out of the sepia mud.
Seeing Jon running towards him, he stood
up into a quarterback stance while he spun

the ball, resting the laces on his fingers
to throw it back to Jon, who stood waiting
with his hands out in the air. Only bad thing
was that this happened also to be the summer

my brother had seen *Cool Hand Luke* one night
on cable, and now was in the habit of calling
everybody "boy," even our mom, as in
"Please pass the Sugar Smacks, boy." So, not

at all aware of the red that colors some words
and seeing the kid about to toss the ball,
Jon yelled out, "Right here, boy." The kid's face fell
from an easy smile, shattering into shards

of hate and hurt. "Nobody calls me boy!"
he spat. And then he chucked the ball for what
to us seemed like a mile down the beach and walked
off toward his buddies, laughing at the way

Jon looked as the ball bounced over to the blue-
gray rocks of the Hampton jetty. Jon dragged his gaze
from the fading older boys to where I was
standing. After some seconds, he jogged to

go get the ball. He walked to where our stuff
was junked in violet patches of chairs and rafts
and blankets. Lines of anger lightly lashed
his face. When he asked me what he'd done to piss

that kid off, all I could tell him was that black
guys didn't like being called "boy," which Jon
didn't believe was a very good reason,
so I told him that it somehow went back

to slave days. That was all I really knew.
Jon's head spun back to where the older kid
had walked, but he was gone, and Jon got stung sad
as a beaten dog. He dropped his olive-green eyes.

He laid down in the sand, a towel his pillow,
and did not get up for hours, but swept the sand
over his legs to bury the flesh of his skin
in tans and maizes that had once been yellow.

A GOOD SLEEP

Maybe it was the floor's
frozen pond of wood
in the room where his bed
rested always made
or maybe it was the bent
and black maple that stared
through him from the window
as if waiting for his eyes
to quit their vigilance
or perhaps it was that,
coming home late, their dad
tripped past his door
on the way to the toilet,
threatening to explain himself
again, but something haunted
him enough that for years
he slept on the floor snug
between his older brothers'
beds in a sleeping bag, risking
their missteps in the dark,
their feet on his head.
This skinny and scared kid
who would wake to throw
a nasty breaking ball, blow up
lines on a blitz, break his egg
for others, find his iron city
flower and tease grass
out of granite, always laughing
for the sake of living with a wink
and grin at the world. This kid
too scared to sleep in his own bed.

MARGIE RAE

I create my mother dancing
in '65 on the corner
sidewalk of Wilder Street
spring straining through
the slabbed concrete
dancing
as she waits
for the downtown bus
to shuttle her
to the high school dancing for
why or who I don't know
but dancing oblivious
in a black wool coat
she must have got
for Christmas dancing
despite the March clouds and
the somber eyes waiting by
her at the bus stop waiting
for the last months
of senior year to wiggle
away into graduation waiting
as my mother's still dancing
waiting to take their slots
in the mills and kitchens
factories and garages florists
and typing pools waiting as
long as they can for
what will be as long
as they are
yet against their postures
my mother is dancing
somehow she is

dancing maybe sensing
a long summer coming
in streets far away to
music far away
she is dancing
because she hasn't yet
been caught
by her dad one night
dancing behind her dinner
and told
You get to go anywhere you want
for college
as long as you're home every night
for dinner
and then he looks away
from her wincing down
a bite of meat loaf
staring past the flaked paint on
the ribs of the kitchen window
seeing the sun leaning
on the spindle hills
and the campus buildings
of Lowell State that shove up
against the sky less than
a mile away and knowing
she will be walking
to class next fall
instead
of dancing in September
at a bus station for
a bus
out of town.

A White Seven Christmas Carol

A bedpan, my bedpan, catches a glint
of the first shoving open of dawn

as the sun breaks light over the Beacon
Hill winter burn, pushing against

Mass. General's White Seven windows.
This is my Christmas, tied down to

monitors with lights colored festive
red and green, with bells and screams

ready to peel if nothing comes down
the shoot, down the J-tube stuck into

my arm with a needle as silver
as a lone strand of tinsel.

This is my Christmas tree, my
IV mount decorated with buttons and

lit plastic switches, with a TPN
food pump tubing into my chest,

and a morphine drip hung with care
inside a plastic stocking.

These are my elves
in the hall, the nurses rolling out on their

hypodermic dawn patrols, whispering
in their scrubs, bringing shiny gifts

to all the boys and girls (good or bad,
we all make the list).

Outside my door
is Santa Claus, or really just a fat guy

in a ski-cap, scraping his plastic slippers
across the floor behind a walker, all of

his toys packed into a colostomy bag
that's leaking through his johnnie.

These are the greedy kids,
the doctors and residents

on rounds, sneaking down to unwrap
their presents.

This is my holiday punch,
my temperature spiking to 106.

This is my angel in the manger,
my wife, putting a cool towel on my head,

and calling my three kings, our boys,
at home, and telling them they

better be good and drive into Boston
right now.

FOURTH OF JULY

Standing up there,
tall in the dunes at night
like shadows in the bonfire fog,
splitting their first stolen
pony of Budweiser,
the two boys, cousins,
thin, blond, tanned,
against the cottage lights,
make a silhouette
of upturned rifles
shoved into the tangle
of crab grass and sand
and topped with the
netted steel of helmets,
as if they were
the quick-made graves
of fallen soldiers.

MORNING SICKNESS

Awake all night, my stomach all unspun, I get dressed again
and climb the roof stairs to a still-dark North End morning
where the wasp star hovers its last barbed wink
over a dawn already bruised with clouds.

Alarm clocks erupt within the walls below,
stirring the commuter bleed of redbrick apartments
as the sun intrudes shadows on the chimneys.
At the bottom of the 4th floor drop I can hear the first click of heels

on Sheafe Street where garbage trucks begin their bang and swallow.
Looking north towards the fade of the moon, I watch traffic copters
mosquito over 93 as headlights thick-stream through the lower deck
then disappear into the Big Dig drilling. My stomach lurches.

Jets rip the air flying in and out of Logan. My hands grab my knees.
In the slanted rooftop puddles the pigeons that drink and bathe
scatter when my dinner splashes near the gutter edge.
My legs shake as I watch the colors bleed off the tar.

I turn back toward the door, let my legs rubber down the steps'
wooden moan, and like a clumsy ghost I bump and haunt the morning
towards the bedroom where my wife still sleeps. I lay down next to her,
curl into her. I rest my hand on her belly swelling over the bed's horizon.

III. winter seeds

QUICKEN

"As you head off for the eternal horizon on your treadmill, you must be aware that this march is almost by definition a waste of time, made possible by the luxury of time, made necessary by the disappearance of backbreaking labor from the daily routine."

—*from* Faster *by James Gleick*

With the grunting lungs of a pulling guard
trying to kick out the d-tackle on a trap
play, Jesus comes running around the corner
of winter, his wheels spinning and mud splashing
across the white clapboard houses as he
gets caught in those flowing robes we've painted on
him and takes a digger into the dirt, coming
up blacker than history. But he's back on
his feet in no time, all jacked up for Easter
services, and he's bounding up the steps of the church
with the zeal of someone who wants to speak now
and never hold his peace, only he punched
in on sidereal as opposed to digital
time which, unknown to heaven, we have slowly
sped up to adjust for forward increments
of work and sex and drugs and pilates. So
the old boy bursts through the oak doors twenty
minutes after the twelfth hour and sees the pews
all empty except maybe for a kung fu-grip
action figure forgotten by some worn-
down mom of an ADD son. And ain't it just
like the Christ, as he takes a seat way in the back
disappointed and more than a little confused,
to show up late for his own resurrection?

Dear Inventor Lover

Dear inventor lover, come poking at me with your knives and tweezers,
　　calibrate my robot deviations with your serrated calipers!
My skin is a film of cracking solar panels rotting with laptop smallpox
　　from an anthrax that swaps spit with wireless hookups!
And my eyes, goddamn my eyes, are burning from the digital
　　belligerence I lean into like a bought boxer or some battered
wife afraid to be left alone with herself. I have nothing left
　　for myself except some hits of E and laughing gas.
Look, my hangnails are loose wires sticking out of fingers all crooked
　　and cracked from scratching at the lid of the casket. I rip
at the wires, tugging circuits and sinew through my weakening
　　widening pores and what's left of my flesh.
Oh, you should see the sparks and fire fly from my hands!
　　I could quicken life in still waters with the lightning leaving me.
I am sad and filthy with flesh! I need to replace myself with
　　plastic struts, with epoxy chemicals, with nanotech nose hairs,
with soft cybernetics and laser optics. Make me a machine!
　　Make me safe for the earth! Tickle my feet with your micro fibers!
Make me small enough to travel on waves of light and firing synapses.
　　Muscle and ligaments have been made redundant by gears and wheels,
which were made obsolete by cable and hypertext then made a memory
　　by tasty psychotropics and finally all of it to be unplugged into nothing
by the snuffing out of the fission and fusion of a fat and cocky sun.
　　So let me be your laboratory! Tinker with me. Replace my parts!
They are only there to rot anyway! Cut me loose into liquid crystal! It's okay.
　　No one is watching anymore. The moon has turned away. Be the pilot
of my improvement. I supplicate myself to you, doctor, to you, scientist,
　　to you, television, to you, professor, to you, weatherman, to you,
cozy mother, to you, coarse lover, to you, memory implant. I want
　　to kiss, you and when I do please pull my tongue out
with your electric pliers. Please, please impart to me your sweet synthetics.
　　Frankenstein me my perfection. I'll name all your beasts.
I am your Adam.

DREAMCATCHER

In the blue blonde morning
as the sun rose to diamond
the dew on the stamps of chain-
linked yards, as the smell of coffee
seeped out from drive-throughs,
the boy went up into the hills
to shoot some Indians. The first
he found in a country bookstore,
the next by the roadside selling
wallets. The last he blasted in the head
shop run by hippies. He shot each
brave in the chest and then ate
their exposed hearts as he knew
from television was their custom.
Then he cleaned and stripped them
of their hides. On the way home he
ghostdanced down the road in blue
moccasins spitting tobacco. Then
he went into town to the market
square to sell dreamcatchers and
airbrushed paintings of horseback
hunters carrying spears and feathers.
In the blue blonde morning the
boy went up into the hills to shoot
some Indians and steal their skin.

AT THE CHADWICK MUSIC FESTIVAL

As if bent by the loom
that wove the blue wool
of her sweater, an old
woman, her skull showing
through a thin nest of hair,
slumps like a collapsed lung
into the cold, unfolded iron
seat of the auditorium
to watch the performance
of a local string quartet.
The house lights dim
around her. The violins
and viola are raised.
Thighs assume the bruises
of the cello, and the four begin
to play. In their thrusts
and cuts, in their callused
dancing across fingerboards,
as their necks and spines
hold hard and fast the angles
to sting and wince a pitched
melody, the old woman tastes
the rain seeded by their lightning.
In swollen pauses and arrests
she hears the shared breaths
between divinity and death.

PLAYING THE MNEMONICA

The violence of memory
like a nest of hornets
built over the back door, like
hips rolling in the sand,
like weak coffee in police stations,
like cheap ties, clip-ons,
patrol car ride alongs,
priests—no, that's too easy.
Philosophies of sarcasm and
cynicism are bled like Drano
from the TV, glass takes over
for skin, crippled engines
with their feet up.
Go ahead, sugar my tank,
I'll start to walk. Tell me
all about the hornets, and
I'll slingshot their paper
homes and watch the frenzy.

DOG DAY

Up Christian Hill, where the Robinson
School leans into the spill of ball
fields, Sirius leashes to the sun
and wags a heat that will hover
this memory over every next

July the twenty-fifth: squirt kids
tear through chalk lines playing soccer
for empty seats unfolded along
the sidelines while two teenagers hump
behind the school as a third laps up

the leftovers of a lowlifed case
of beer waiting her turn as she
throws fireworks in the dumpster and
then shudders at the bang. Up by
the swings and underneath an iron

slide a little girl comes across a book
of matches and learns how to burn
them down to her thumb and cry
at the way it stinks in her hair. Until
her mom hugs and scolds her all the way

to the wailing bark of carnival
music that loops from an ice cream truck
cracking into crazy an ice cream man.
He sweats inside his house of rolling
tin, passing bomb pops to a bunch

of middle-aged men just off the court
whom he thinks look like a bunch of sniffs
the way they lope across the park,
their tongues hanging in laughter. And no
one notices a boy hopping

over a chain-link fence into
a backyard overgrown with weeds
and ivy to pet an unchained sleeping
pit bull. The dog stirs when the boy nears,
and wakes with a sudden eruption of God.

LAUGHTER FROM THE BASKET

The scream of a child broke through the line
of trees, stopping everyone like clumsy thieves
in the middle of their lives. Whether the voice
belonged to a girl or boy no one could really say
If anyone had the nerve to speak, that is, which none
did. For the pain in the scream seemed to make
even the branches of the maples and elms seize
in terror, to make the stones suddenly conscious
of time, to make men and women busying through
the park hurt somewhere deep and pink, somewhere
where they were still young and smooth skinned.
And then, like all screams, this scream stopped.
It was barely seconds before all their eyes
began to meet, as if trying to recognize friends
they had played with behind these grown-up jaws
and jowls. Some of the sterner shook themselves
free of terror. They tried to seek the source
of the scream. Others began to nod and follow
them. Weaker spirits dropped their heads and stayed
along the path. Regardless, the child was never
found. Nor was anyone ever sure after whether
it had been a child. Maybe it had been a bird
or some strange bug. Some began to talk
themselves out of having ever heard anything
at all. None of these answers worked for long.
The scream had come from a child, and the child
was gone after the scream, and the people who heard
it would always hear it, in their thoughts, in their
breaths. And they couldn't help but give voice
to it in their own words and songs, no matter
how much they tried to shut it out. And the scream
spread like germs from mouth to mouth beyond

the park, the town, the state, the nation. It swarmed
the earth like some last plague of locusts until
there was not one set of eyes or ears or hands left
that was not working through its own death.

ELEVENS

"Where like Arion on the dolphin's back
I saw him hold acquaintance with the waves"
                    —-from Twelfth Night

"About 4-5 feet, water temp 62°, clean and glassy conditions, a slight offshore
breeze."
                    —New Hampshire Surf Report at 6 PM on 9/11/01

Waves, head high and whispered off the lips
of Hurricane Ellen, with faces like blown glass,

with bellies like thunder, push over the dusk
coast of New Hampshire as sun-stained clouds

hemorrhage across a cobalt west and September
leans back for its lazy late-inning throws of summer.

A surfer paddles out, duck-dives the stampeding
whales of chop that crush above the sea floor.

His face stings in the salt and cold as he pierces through
the backs of the waves until finally past the shore break

he sits up and stares for a set to horizon against the east.
Just seconds and then surging up like a mountain

of shadows, a wave catches him in its steep pull.
Spray kicks up as he slices down its glassing face. He pops

up to his feet, crouches into the curl, carving a
bottom turn and forgetting or not needing to breathe

as he slides back up the wall that's tumbling into foam
inches behind him, and there's no such thing as thinking,

just going with the wave as it dips and rises, dies
and resurges, coaxes him into tucks and nose-walks,

speeds him up, slows him down, covers him up in rumbled
laughter, the whole world becoming soluble in water.

And then he pulls out, off the gently lowered shoulder,
and paddles out again. He turns and stares back

toward the shore. He watches the day drip down into a
nuclear sunset behind the power-plant standing in

the marshes behind the rows of suppertime cottages,
where he knows inside all of the TV sets hum

and glow with the fire and fall of steel choking a
skyline only a few hours south, a skyline set above

this same sea that rolls in and out without account,
untouched by memory, with no reason to forget.

THE LOOP

whispers against the dark then light flickers,
fades in. master cut, tracking shot, focus
on boots and flannel, on winds ripping in all
bearded with frost, on ice that cuts across
your face like storm-torn wires still snapping alive
from the local invisible, light and power.
december. pale sun. naked earth and ozone,
and you begin your plot against the giant,
but you are the giant, you are. you are the bull,
the boy, in the china-plate maze feeding on time,
chasing the twine—but enough rhetoric.
stop exposition, composition—get back
in scene. show, don't...show. don't. and sell
the scene: the air was cold enough to kill
small birds sideways on the sidewalk that
you stomp on your way to get a tin of dip,
a coffee, smokes, diet pills or sudafed
and then you *go down to the river and into*
the river you see the dead blonde and blown reeds
of the salt marsh standing in the TV screen
water and looking like the spiky tufts
of a drowned giant, but wait you are the giant
and *here we go, here we go, here we go*
again, what's the subject? amen as you hunch
into a bench along the riverwalk,
isolated by that article "the," single giant,
lone aberration, no more monsters left
to ragnarok around the clock with just
the ax and the eyes, blue eyes, *where have you gone*
my blue viking iris? you're the last thickback
krautmicfriendly waiting by the sea for the boats,
those dragon ships arriving on blossoms

of fire, skaldic poets and etheridge
knights pounding beer guts into belly songs,
blood rhythms, scented beats, and raven chants,
and suddenly you feel the daemon in
your craw, got you going faster than surf
guitar, and now it's not december after
all—august has risen and it's muscled with swans
and the sun is not sick after all—look, the wax
is melting off the wings and off the boards
and you start slipping out of the air into
all the *oh, baby, baby, what a wild world* ears
pinned back as you prepare to crash as you splash
into the sea mouth of the merrimack
caught in ribbons, caught in candy, tangled
in currents, and the water is as cold
and salty as thecenterofdeath because
it is not summer after all, but it is
not death after all and all is humming on,
rolling along a playback loop inside
the projection booth, and all is born again
again from this winter seed and ecstasy.

THE MUTE

And he to me: These miserable ways
The forlorn spirits endure of those who spent
Life without infamy and without praise

They are mingled with that caitiff regiment
Of the angels, who rebelled not, yet avowed
To God no loyalty, on themselves intent.
                    —*from* The Inferno, Canto III

There are no boots marching, no steel
toes knocking at my door, no black coats
coming to arrest me, and yet I have stopped
in the middle of the song, turned quiet
at my turn. The scopes on the roofs are
not on me, they are not even my roofs,
and still nothing, no rhythm hung lyrics,
not even humming or whistling
against evening graveyards. Why am I
unbound yet so silent? Why, not yet tied
by bars or knives, with mud or dung
beetles, not soiled in search lights and
rusty puddles, am I so mute, so dumb?
So uncensored, why do I wither all
my untethered hours lying in the sand
by the summer sea? Horseflies chew
the salt from my skin, and I do nothing.

a cknowledgements

The author is grateful to the editors and publishers of the following publications in which some of these poems—some of which have been revised—first appeared.

Connecticut Review: "The Blades" and "Morning Sickness"; *Entelechy International:* "The Loop," "Periscope," and "Playing the Mnemonica"; *Beacon Street Review:* "Piscatory Diner"; *Renovation Journal:* "The Mute," "Coloring," "Mechanics," and "White Seven Christmas"; *The Offering:* "Dear Inventor Lover," "The Plows," and "Yucca Hunters"; *Henniker Review:* "Conjunction"; *Third Coast:* "Hierarchy of Paradise."

"Coloring," "The Blades," and "Hierarchy of Paradise" were featured on *Sunrise* on WUML, 91.5, UMass Lowell. "Gravediggers Union" was selected as a featured poem for the Whistler House Museum of Art's *Evening of Poetry*, sponsored by the Lowell Hellenic Institute, in September 2004.

This book would not have been possible without the support of friends and family including: my wife, Emily Meehan, and my daughter, Delaney; my parents, Marge and Frank Miller, my brother Jon and his wife Stacey; my brother Paul, his wife Laura and their daughter Sierra; Betty, Eddy, and the whole Dick clan; Ray, Rosanne, and Sage Riddick; Gram and Coach Riddick; Joe and Nancy Meehan; David O. Robinson and Melissa Spead; Joe Hurka; the Freshmen Bullpups; Basile, Jozoks, Spitzy and G-Man; Paul Marion and Loom Press; Vicky Dalis, Meghan Moore, and Mary Lou Hubbell; and the city and citizens of Lowell. A very special thanks as well to John Skoyles, Alison Matika, Bill Knott, Mary Peterson, Maura Macneil, Martha Donovan, Lisa Gilmore, Gail Mazur, Sam Cornish, Carm Cozza, Kevin Slattery, Greg McAdams, Major Jackson, Michael Hoerman, Kate and Denny at *Renovation Journal* and the Lowell Poetry Network.

a bout the author

Matt Miller was born in Lowell, Massachusetts in 1973. He played
football at Yale University and earned an M.F.A. in Creative Writing
from Emerson College. He worked as a landscaper, security guard,
window blind installer, and freelance reporter before becoming a
Lecturer in Writing at New England College and a staff writer for
the University of Massachusetts Lowell. His work has appeared in
*Connecticut Review, Entelechy International, Beacon Street Review,
Henniker Review, The Offering*, and *Renovation Journal*. He has
received a Mogan Cultural Center grant from Lowell National
Historical Park and was twice nominated for a Pushcart Prize. A
Wallace Stegner Fellow in Poetry at Stanford University, he makes his
home in Lowell with his wife, Emily Meehan, and their daughter,
Delaney.